Welcome Home – Simply Country

by
Judy Condon

Library of Congress Cataloging-in-Publications Data
Welcome Home - Simply Country by Judy Condon
ISBN 978-0-9772309-6-9

Oceanic Graphic Printing, Inc.
105 Main Street
Hackensack, NJ 07601

Printed in China

Layout and Design by Pat Lucas

About the Author

Judy Condon is a native New Englander, which is evident in her decorating style and the type of antiques she collects and sells. Her real passion is 19thC authentic dry red or blue painted pieces. While Judy's professional career evolved as a teacher, Principal and Superintendent of Schools in Connecticut, Judy's weekends were spent at her antique shop, Marsh Homestead Country Antiques, located in Litchfield, Connecticut.

When her husband, Jeff, was relocated to Virginia, Judy accepted an early retirement from education and concentrated her energy and passion for antiques into a fulltime business. Judy maintains a website, http//www.marshhomesteadantiques.com and has been a Power Seller on eBay® for over eleven years under the name "superct".

With the success of her books and her working relationships with country shops throughout the United States and Canada, Judy has created a successful wholesale business featuring hand-poured primitive wax pieces and other handmade country accessories that she sells wholesale to country shops.

Judy has five children and five grandchildren and lives in Spotsylvania, Virginia with her husband Jeff.

Judy's first six books in the "simply country" series, *Country on a Shoestring, Of Hearth and Home – Simply Country, A Simpler Time, Country Decorating for All Seasons, As Time Goes By* and *Country at Heart* have been instant hits. Judy may be reached through her website or her email address, marshhomestead@comcast.net

Introduction

Many of you have asked if I would include pictures of the exterior of homes and perhaps even country gardens. As a result of your requests, I've changed the format of this book and will continue the "simply country" series with this new format I call "house tours".

While I enjoy visiting homes and photographing the decorating talents each homeowner demonstrates, the greater joy is in meeting the people who live in the homes. When my first book was published, I was contacted by a young eighty-year-old woman named Billy Lowry of Alabama who couldn't wait to receive my first book and, as she said, "any other book you write". Over the past year or so, I've come to enjoy her sense of humor as our paths continue to cross with the availability of each new book.

After the completion of my fourth book, one day I was surprised to receive a package from Billy with a lovely note attached. The package contained a framed poem and a handwritten letter that said, in part, "I know your mother said 'you can't fit another thing in this house'; maybe you can find an empty wall for this poem I found many years ago in a book. My mama would say 'please don't buy anything else'. One year I thought she was going to have to hold the Christmas tree in her lap till January as there was just no place to put it. Thanks Judy for all the good pictures and reading. If another hurricane comes, I'll grab my four good books, and the dog and run". Billy is but one of the many new friends who have become part of my life as a result of the "simply country" series.

Our unique styles and individual decorating are the loving thumbprints we leave behind. Each home pictured in *Welcome Home – Simply Country* reflects those thumbprints and "the heart that gives its love".

Poem sent by Billy Lowry

> *He who loves an old house, Will never love in vain*
> *For how can any old house, Used to sun and rain,*
> *To lilac and to larkspur, To arching trees above,*
> *Fail to give its answer, To the heart that gives its love.*

In this book, you will also meet Lovey Makepeace whose love of history and an extraordinary imagination have brought great enjoyment to me and to all those with whom I've shared "her story".

Table of Contents

Chapter 1

✦ ▦ ✦

Carl and Randy Oliverio

Many years ago, I had the pleasure of meeting Carl Oliverio but had never visited his home that he shares with his wife, Randy. Carl and Randy opted fifteen years ago to leave the fast paced life of the Connecticut "gold coast" and head west. They settled in a small village just northeast of Columbus in a home on Maple Street. The house, built in 1840 was the dairy farm for the village and was a Victorian style with large picture windows across the front. Randy and Carl had the foresight to imagine what the house would look like when restored to period. One of the first things they did was to remove the large glass windows and replace them with nine-over nine paned windows. They added the fireplace in the living room, pictured on the top of the next page, which is the first room to the right off the center hall.

The portrait of a Connecticut minister over the mantel is dated 1792. Carl likes the fact that it is a profile. The make-do chair to the left of the mantel is from America Home Division, one of three divisions of Carl's business.

In the corner to the right of the mantel, the one piece New Hampshire red Stepback dates to the 1830's. The small paint decorated blue stool was found in Maine. Sitting on top is a whale oil lantern, also from Maine. The coverlet is Ohio and is signed and dated 1833. Carl purchased the entire stack of boxes shown right from an estate in Maine. The lantern on top is a screened cricket box. The heart mold in front of the middle box is made of wood and was given as a gift. Two early Massachusetts silhouettes hang on the wall above

The wooden standing candle stand is one item, which Carl replicates and sells in his business. It stands before a 19thC Connecticut mule chest in dry red paint. Two 18thC samplers framed in gold hang above. One of the samplers was a housewarming gift from the owner of a Connecticut home Carl and Randy purchased.

The Maine circa 1840's cupboard pictured left is one of Carl's favorites because of its large size. It is filled with some of Carl and Randy's extensive pewter collection. Carl won't buy a piece of pewter unless it has an American tax stamp on the back. In the 18thC, Colonists were expected to turn their pewter in to be melted down for artillery. If they refused, the tax collector would stamp the back. Each year a different stamp was used and the age of a piece of pewter can be determined by the number of stamps on the back and the type of stamp used.

Carl and Randy found the 1850's table with robin's egg blue paint in Westport Connecticut. The deacon's bench next to it dates to the 1820's. A large pine trencher filled with Granny Smith apples sits on the table in the center. Early wedding band hogscrapers can be seen at the edge of the photo. An early spoon rack hangs in the corner of the dining room opposite a Colorado twig wreath.

The Connecticut 1760's cupboard pictured left is Carl's favorite piece. It is filled with

pewter and tin ware. The blue painted box on top is actually a sewing box and has an attached yardstick on the top.

A hanging shelf over the dry sink holds a collection of measures and a heart in hand make-do.

Leaning against the wall on the sill are pockets holding small handmade candles used as lighters.

I think the sunlight streaming through the window accentuates the beauty of the 19thC Maine dry sink with red paint.

Some of Carl and Randy's dough bowls in original paint are displayed on the wall leading to the kitchen.

Pictured on page 11, across the back of the house, the working kitchen area revolves around a large mustard island found in New York City. It houses the stove and oven on the backside. At the opposite end of the room, Carl and Randy converted a large bathroom area into a dining area. The beam shown in the top of the picture was added when the wall was removed to open up the two rooms. The bench at the end is one of a pair owned by Randy's grandmother Nellie.

A Maine 1850's chimney cupboard with a tombstone cutout top can be seen in the background.

The oxblood red painted cupboard holds spices.

Using an old door, Carl and Randy constructed a two-door panel to hide their refrigerator. Sitting on top of the small hanging cupboard is a wooden tea caddy.

Pictured below right, a collection of old and new red ware is displayed in the 1850's cupboard from Maine. The curtain on the bottom hides the microwave.

Pictured below left, the blue bucket bench found in Ohio dating to the mid 19thC brightens up a space under the window and matches the blue in the vintage homespun curtains. Cheesecloth covers on early painted buckets add an additional element of age to the space.

At the other end of the back of the house, Carl and Randy added the 5' X 5' fireplace, which they use for cooking. The pot rack, barely visible on the right side of the photo left is their earliest piece dating to 1690. A hunt board over the fireplace opening holds candles. Suspended in the foreground of the photo from the top of the fireplace opening is a hen cooker. It has a key that is used to wind it up and it rotates to cook the hen. The piece dates to the late 19thC.

Pictured below right, Carl found the tin crow on top of the open blue chimney cupboard in Connecticut. The brooms pictured to the right of the cupboard are made of olive branches.

The folk art log home is early and was a gift from friends. The early feed sack holds corn. Below left, the tin star cookie cutter was found in Ohio.

The bathroom, shown below right, was converted from a mudroom. Carl and Randy used an old apple green florist stand to house the brass sink. A wooden candy mold of a crow sits on the shelf above the sink. An old feed sack remnant serves as a hand towel.

Pictured on page 17, the schoolmaster's desk is Connecticut and dates to the 1820's. The Windsor chair is DR Dimes. The cupboard pictured against the wall is pumpkin pine and was found in Maine. It is circa 1830's. On the top sits an 18thC oil lamp from New England.

Pictured above, the room to the left of the front entranceway is done in mustards with red accents.

A large trencher filled with apples sits atop the early six-board chest from Maine.

The custom made cabinet above right is one that is offered from Carl's America Home Division. In addition to Carl's shop, America Antiques, located in Newark Ohio, Carl custom designs and makes replicas of early pieces. Carl's third division offers curtains, bed linens, candles and other small country accessories. A funnel candlestick is seen on the top of the cupboard. On the table in the foreground of the photo is an early-screened cricket lantern.

Pictured below, the stairway is lined with early painted game boards.

A colorful stack of painted boxes is placed on the landing at the top of the stairs.

On the second floor landing, a tin folk art angel, made by a local artisan, is silhouetted in front of the window.

The hooked rug over the early bed was hooked by a local artisan. The linens are from America Home Division, as are the paper boxes shown below and the child's horse.

Sitting on the small drop leaf table is an 1850's document box.

The small table in front of the window is actually an early cobbler's bench.

An old farrier's carrier serves as a wall shelf over the bed in the guest room.

The 1850's two-door cupboard in old English brown paint holds an early chest and paper boxes. A large stack of painted stools stands in front of the window.

After I finished photographing the inside of Carl and Randy's home, we sat outside on their back porch to enjoy what was left of a glorious comfortable August day. While we sipped ice tea, we looked over the herb garden enclosed with a wonderful old gate with heart cutout.

To the right of the brick path, Carl and Randy have numerous garden beds filled with a wide variety of flowers and accented with vintage birdhouses and garden accessories.

At the end of the path we arrived at a secluded area with the table set for dining. Carl and Randy eat in this quiet spot almost every night in the summer months.

It seemed to be the perfect spot to end a perfect visit and wonderful experience of photographing Carl and Randy's lovely home.

Chapter 2

❧ ✿ ❧

Bob and Criss Cefus

A remnant of an early nameless headstone containing what may be a shamrock is nestled in the beds of impatiens leading up to the door.

It was late in the day and I was trying to beat darkness as I drove north two and a half hours from Columbus in a light rain. As I arrived at the home of Bob and Criss Cefus, the rain let up and I decided I would take advantage of the lull in the weather and the last bit of light to photograph the spectacular gardens surrounding their 1876 home. The property was originally owned by a man named Memmer, a farmer with huge orchards of apples. Even after Bob and Criss moved to the home in 1986, occasionally passer-bys would stop and ask if they were selling any cider or apple butter.

The house needed extensive restoration but as Criss reported "it had good bones". Bob and Criss ripped up tiles, carpet, and removed wallpaper to achieve the look they now have. In 1995 they purchased an 1830's log home, used as a tobacco barn in northern North Carolina and moved it to Ohio. Bob, a retired chemist, did much of the work himself, starting in the dead of winter to stack the logs and add windows and a fireplace. In 1996, they added the buttr'y that connects the main house with the log home.

We entered the house into the kitchen area.

The log cabin addition is seen from the beds of coneflowers and black-eyed Susans.

Criss found the 19thC hutch table with original red paint in the basement of a Pennsylvania farmhouse. The underneath of the table was dry scraped to reveal remnants of mustard, red and salmon paint. Criss purchased the early settle at a local auction.

Criss has utilized every available space including that surrounding the window over the kitchen sink. A collection of ovoid and storage crocks circles a row of early red ware. The two crocks, top right, were made by a local potter. The lantern is a newly made electrified piece.

The shelf shown above is early and contains treen cups and salt cellars.

The armchair dates to circa 1680 and is New England.

Criss aged her walls throughout the house by using a water base burnt umber paint which she mixed with water and applied with a sponge.

Shelves to the right of the door hold trenchers and on the bottom shelf left a rare burl dipper.

The tall Stepback is early 19thC and houses some of Criss' extensive red ware collection. Pictured on the bottom shelf is an onion bottle and early New England herb grinder from Vermont.

Bob and Criss added the mantel and fireboard. The 18thC storage barrel on the floor has a button band on the top made of wood. The small hanging red cupboard is New England.

The Pennsylvania lantern is 18thC and is illuminated with a battery powered LED taper.

A small 1830's drop front desk sits tucked in a corner of the alcove in the kitchen. It is initialed on the inside and says "Starr, PA".

Criss hand painted the tree behind the camel back sofa and on other walls in the stairwell. Throughout the house, Bob and Criss have placed hanging butterys to achieve greater display space.

The gray corner cupboard is very late 1700's and is from New England. The smaller of the two wallpaper boxes is signed and from Ohio. On top of the cupboard rests a New England 18thC decorated chest. An early wooden barn lantern hangs above. An early trammel with candlestick is suspended from the top of the cupboard.

A number of years ago, the local historical society was interested in disposing of many of the leather bound Bibles it had accumulated. Criss was fortunate to be able to purchase a great number of them at a reasonable price.

The small hanging red cupboard is New England and has original HL hinges on the inside.

The candlestick below it holds an early wooden rush light.

A small alcove holds more leather books and an early courting or spiral candlestick.

The clock is 1820's from Connecticut. Resting on the table next to the rush light is the earliest Bible Criss and Bob own. It is dated 1703.

The tavern table with stretcher base is mid 18thC and is mustard over red paint.

The hanging shelf contains small wallpaper boxes and early red chest with snipe hinges between two diminutive chests in paint.

The ladder back chair with sausage turning is 18thC.

The large corner cupboard in blue paint has chamfered doors and is pinned. It was found in Georgia and originally held smoked hams. The piece on top is an early red with black sponge decorated chest.

Hanging in the doorway leading into the sitting room, the early tin lantern has horn panels rather than glass and may be English. The horn was worn down and boiled to make it thin enough to be transparent. The use of horn precedes the use of glass in early lighting.

An enclosed porch at the far end of the sitting room overlooks the gardens and small pond pictured at the end of the chapter.

The sawbuck table with X base is unusual in that the top lifts up and folds down. An early table rug covers the top and holds a make do wooden base and iron rush light.

The 19thC red painted lift top chest in the corner holds an early Bible box with the date 1723 carved on top. A small child's fraktur, most likely of Pennsylvania origin is hanging on the wall in the corner.

Once again utilizing a hanging butt'ry, the shelf holds a collection of early lighting including a witch's hat lantern and a large whale oil lamp.

The early oil portrait depicts a physician with his stethoscope around his neck.

For the past few years, Bob and Criss have created and sent holiday greeting cards they personally create. This is the last year of the Scrooge series and I've included their first card using the desk pictured left with Bob in costume.

The message inside the card says "You're definitely not on my gift list this year, but here's a card anyway.... Bah Humbug!!!"

The oval pocket on the side is an early spill holder filled with small lighters. Above the mantel hangs an early tin lantern with wooden base.

A small double hanging Betty lamp hangs to the right of the fireplace from a branch hook.

In the corner is an 18thC child's settle in red with a dove tailed single board seat. The seat pulls out for storage. Above it a small New England red painted cupboard fills the space in the corner. It was most likely a built-in at one time.

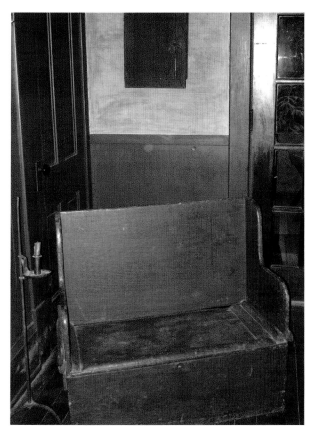

Leading from the parlor, I stepped into another century through a buttr'y entrance to the log cabin addition. The butttr'y was filled on every wall and nook with one delightful collectible after another.

Straight ahead a trencher holds some of the gourds Criss grows in her garden and sells each year. These gourds are called spinning top gourds. This past year she grew and sold birdhouse gourds. Two years ago Criss grew gourds which she crafted into "gourd spoons". To the right of the gourds, is a stone soap dish. Hanging on the wall is a diminutive wall box. Criss made the gourd ladle at the end of the shelf.

Pictured top right, a shelf above the early stone sink holds pantry boxes on the first shelf. The gray box on the right is marked Mt. Lebanon and is Shaker. On the top shelf, a collection of baskets and a tin sugar sit below a larger shelf with red ware including a large red ware milk bowl.

The hanging wisk to the left of the sink is made from twisted branches.

Firkins, treenware, crocks, red ware and pontilled storage jars line the shelves on the far side of the butt'ry. An early herb grinder is on the top shelf.

Atop the little spice chest hanging on the wall, tin shakers are placed in a row.

Pictured above is the view as you enter the log cabin. An adjustable trammel candleholder is suspended from the ceiling.

Pictured below, the settle to the right of the fireplace was lime green when Bob and Criss found it. Criss was able to scrape it down and clean it up after hours of work. She knew it was the ideal piece for the cabin and wasn't deterred from buying it because of the paint.

Pictured right, the early gray cupboard holds a collection of stone mortar and pestles. The folk art log home on the top dates to the late 1800s.

The hanging nightgown in the corner was found in Pennsylvania. Hanging next to it is an early broom made of corn husks. The hanging broom is possibly Shaker.

The table below left is an unusual wall table so constructed to save space in a small room. The shelf above it holds leather jars possibly used for holding spices and perhaps of Native American Indian origin. A container holding horn spoons is seen on the first shelf at the far left. Pictured with the leather jars is a collection of small snuff boxes.

A New England red painted wall box holds lantern lighters. Below left, a birch dipper, possibly Native American Indian, hangs to the right of two early powder horns.

Pictured below right, an early apple dryer hangs on the wall above a vintage spinning wheel. These apple dryers were customarily hung over the fireplace to dry the apples.

The divining rod on the left side of the window belonged to Criss'
aunt and uncle and was used on their farm. An assortment of breads
and pies cool on the shelf beneath the window. An apple corer can be
seen to the far right on the shelf.

Criss prefers to keep the bedrooms sparsely decorated in soothing earth tones.
Pictured left, a tool to tighten the rope on the bed sits on the trundle bed.

Criss uses unique birdhouses and garden accessories throughout the grounds. Scattered throughout are twig arbors and fences. Criss has a total of eight arbors which includes two arbors of bittersweet. Criss picks and sells bunches of bittersweet each year. There are five grape arbors and one hops arbor.

The enclosed herb garden on the west side of the property contains a variety of early stone troughs and decorative pieces.

Criss and Bob found the stone heads in South Carolina. They resemble the Easter Island figures.

The potting shed on the edge of the driveway was used as the original fruit stand. Walking to the left of it, we entered a huge area of cultivated fruit and flower gardens.

Behind the potting shed, a birdhouse peeks out amidst the marsh grass still covered with dew from the recent showers.

The flower beds were endless with each one adorned with an early birdhouse or figure.

A box of impatiens is suspended to the right of the outbuilding door. Gourds, grown by Criss, hang on the other side. I find the beauty of this picture so soothing that it leaves me almost breathless.

The small pond is filled with fish and is surrounded by an arbor of bittersweet vines.

I was just putting my camera away as I reached my car in the driveway and turned to take one last picture. The sun had just broken through the clouds, the grass was still wet from the rain and there was just a hint of mist rising from the gardens as I snapped the last picture.

Chapter 3

Donna and Mike Perry

Found bordering on the Commons in Woodstock, Connecticut, McClellan Elms is the original home of Samuel McClellan and the current home of Donna and Mike Perry. It is also the location of the Perry's antique shop by the same name. Samuel McClellan, a Revolutionary War general, raised horses on his property for General Washington's army and also commanded a regiment of soldiers at Bunker Hill. When he and two sons left to go to war, Samuel McClellan's wife, Rachel, planted three elms, which for two hundred years grew on the property until the 1950's when the elm tree blight killed them - thus the name McClellan Elms. The main part of the house which houses the large five-room shop was built around 1757. As often was the case, parts were added on to the house and the second part was finished sometime after 1780.

A side entrance is surrounded with perennials and a hydrangea. The paint color on the house is a Sherwin Williams paint named Pennywise. It closely resembles the original color but is a slightly lighter pumpkin color than the original.

A smaller building on the property, reportedly once a general store is being made into a second antique shop.

The shop is entered through the 18thC shed. A winnower in dry blue paint sits in front.

Just outside the entrance to the shop, a wicker table set under a large maple tree overlooks grounds and gardens in the back.

The early grinder and basket filled with bittersweet adorn the open passage from the shed to the shop.

Upon entering the house from the back, the cozy entranceway holds a Hudson River Valley cupboard with original paint. The cupboard came out of a house in Newcastle Maine and is a good example of a primitive make-do to amend the space above the door. An assembled graduated set of seaweed-decorated yellowware sits on the top.

Pictured below, an early sorting tray in mustard paint rests in the well of a dark green painted dry sink. A peel with great surface hangs above it.

The standing dough box with red wash and scrub top was found in Pennsylvania. Sitting on top of it is a square nailed apple box with canted sides holding small pumpkin gourds.

The McClellan house has been used for many purposes over the years. Prior to Mike and Donna purchasing the home, it had been a restaurant and as a result of that, Mike and Donna had to make major renovations to the kitchen area.

The large Hudson River Valley cupboard more resembles a kas. It was found in upstate New York and is a recent acquisition. An early crock with a salt glazed bird is seen at one end. At the far end, a jug with a unique feather and crown pattern is barely visible.

The early trade sign of the running horse on the mantel was found in Maine. In front of the fireplace sits a large tub with dry blue paint and an early bench-made Windsor armchair with a unique form.

Sitting on the six-board early chest under the window is an early grain-painted spoon holder. A schoolhouse clock from Massachusetts made of rosewood with inlays hangs to the left of the window.

The small hallway at the foot of the back stairs is the ideal location for the early 1700 William and Mary reproduction feather painted chest. It has bun feet and is a copy of one that was in the American Folk Art Museum at one time. The lift top desk on top is grain painted and is circa 1825-1840.

Two 1835 oil on wood panel portraits by Zedekiah Belknap hang above the camelback sofa in the Keeping Room. The portraits are of William Cleveland, a sea captain out of Massachusetts and his wife Lucy.

Pictured above, the six-board chest in front of the sofa is grain painted. A candle box in blue paint sits atop an early penny rug.

Below, an early 19thC open Stepback cupboard with gray paint holds some of Mike and Donna's collection of mortar and pestles. The cupboard is pine and is constructed with rose head nails.

Above, a paint decorated black and white dovetailed document box sits on top of a circa 1780 Chippendale soldier blue chest with original snipe hinges. The painting above it is attributed to William Matthew Prior.

Ezrah Ames of Albany, New York painted the portraits of George Smith and his wife, Sarah Cady-Smith pictured to the right of the large red wash cupboard. The Hepplewhite pine table below the portrait is circa 1835 and grain painted.

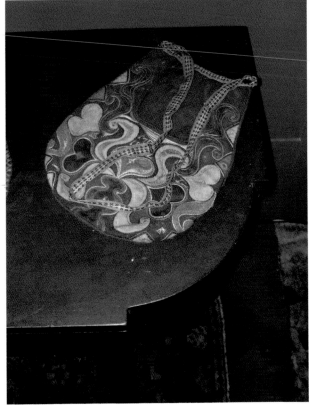

An early turned treen bowl filled with stone fruit is placed next to a recently acquired lady's pocket purse usually tied around the waist. The purse is made of leather and suede and dated 1852. It has an original tape loomed strap and was purchased at a New Hampshire show.

Three early watercolor portraits with original frames hang to the left of the cupboard.

Shown right, the corner cupboard is early New England with a great wave shaped cornice and skirt. Pictured on the top and bottom shelves are ironstone compotes.

A William Matthew Prior portrait is flanked by three mortar and pestles and an assembled graduated set of early pewter chargers. The hanging wooden folk art whale is from a weathervane. The continuous arm Windsor chair is circa 1780 and Rhode Island. The early 18thC dome top chest on the hearth rests behind a pair of leather lady's shoes with hand-carved bases found in Maine.

An assembled set of six different period Windsor chairs surround a 6' long harvest drop leaf table with turned legs.

The hollow cut silhouettes are signed Peale and are of Charles Chamberlain and his wife Sarah. The provenance shows that Charles was born in 1737 and died in 1804. The folk art watercolor to the right on the top shelf reads Asa Hurlburt Farmington Connecticut on the back. The early 19thC miniature watercolor pictured to the left is early 19thC and is of a woman with bonnet.

The table cover, purchased from Bobbie Preiss Antiques of Ohio is block printed, appliquéd then embroidered.

Donna's collection of early hooked mittens and mitten forms sits in the center of the table in a large early trencher.

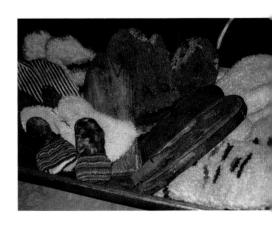

A Pennsylvania Stepback with mustard grain paint circa 1825-1850 is placed at the opposite wall of the dining area from the mantel. The inside of the cupboard retains its original salmon paint.

The circa 1840 watercolor of a young woman in a red dress with a necklace is in its original frame. Shown below it, an early Shaker oval pantry box has been painted with a pattern indicative of a Pennsylvania origin.

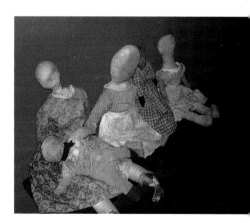

Pictured left, the full-length profile of the watercolor shown left is unsigned but attributed to J Evans who painted out of the Maine seacoast. It has a chamfered backboard and is in its original frame.

Two profile silhouettes of Guinea fowl add an interesting visual to the dovetailed box with snipe hinges found in West Townsend, Massachusetts.

All of the dolls are period 19thC cloth dolls; the smallest of which is an Amish doll which shows signs of being well loved.

The second doll from the right is a topsy-turvy doll with a head at one end and a bear at the other.

A William Mathew Prior hangs above the bed in the master bedroom. Vintage nightdresses hang on the wall to the right of the bed.

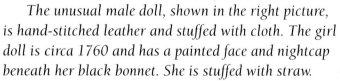

William Jennys, circa 1780-1790 painted the two portraits above left. They hang above a Windsor arrow-back adult chamber chair.

The unusual male doll, shown in the right picture, is hand-stitched leather and stuffed with cloth. The girl doll is circa 1760 and has a painted face and nightcap beneath her black bonnet. She is stuffed with straw.

Pictured left, two Greiner dolls are seated to the left of an early black cloth doll on a black and red pine paint decorated potty-chair.

A rare bedpost doll, circa 1840, is on the far right side.

The built-in highboy is the only documented piece of this kind in eastern Connecticut. It is made of birch and is listed in the Wallace-Nutting furniture registry. The cornice on the highboy is the same molding as the crown molding around the room.

Donna made the bedspread on the early spool bed in one of the guest rooms from a kit. After stenciling wreathes of flowers and hearts, Donna made a series of small tied knots to create the pattern of additional wreaths and hearts. This process is called candlewicking. Donna's sister, Vicci Amato, made the dolls on the bed. The doll on the right holds an early Steiff pull toy.

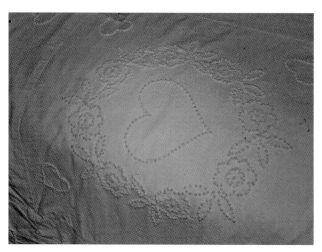

A 19thC Jacquard coverlet is draped across the foot of the early cannonball rope bed in the second guest room. A red and black grain painted blanket chest at the foot of the bed was found in New Jersey.

Pictured right, 19thC painter J G Coles painted the husband and wife portraits above the Sheridan chair and tilt-top table.

Donna and Mike's shop is almost as large as the entire first floor of their home. In addition to five rooms of early country antiques, folk art, Americana in original condition and early 19thC portraits, Donna and Mike sell out of their home as well.

Pictured right, a unique prayer box with a folk artist painted kneeler is but one of the eclectic pieces found at McClellan Elms Antiques in Woodstock Connecticut.

Chapter 4

❧ ✤ ❧

John and Joy Henson

So obscured was the Henson's home by trees and shrubs, I drove for at least five miles before I realized I had missed the house. By the time I found it, Joy Henson was waiting for me in the driveway and gave me a warm welcome as she tried to hold on to her new Spaniel puppy. Joy and her husband John purchased their 1860's home in Ohio in 1978. It had been abandoned and had remained vacant for a number of years. The house had no furnace, water, septic or electricity when Joy and John purchased it. They installed an oil furnace which Joy says they seldom use because heating their house is like heating a tent. They also added a well and a septic system but they have remained essentially without electricity in the majority of the house. The barn pictured above was one Joy and John had built as the original barn stood across the road and simply blew over one day in a windstorm. According to Joy, this was very disconcerting since the barn and house were built the same year. It was not until I entered the house that I came to appreciate the sign over the barn – Olde Thyme Tavern.

Walking along a narrow path through what I called a self-seeding garden but which Joy calls a "happening" as it "just happens", we entered a recently fenced area to keep the new puppy confined; an area which Joy called the 'door yard'. A sign next to the door said "Olde Thyme Tavern".

When I entered the Henson home, not only did I experience first hand what it must have felt like to visit an early 19thC tavern, I found I was no longer speaking with Joy Henson, but rather her reenactment character, Lovey Makepeace.

Lovey proceeded to tell me about the Olde Thyme Tavern and explained that the tavern was an area where wagoners or even sometimes locals, would visit to drink, write letters, and read maps. Indians would come in to trade their furs.

Pictured left, a map showing the surrounding area is posted below a pegged board where there hangs, among other frontier pieces, a buffalo purse often carried by men when they were out hunting the frontier. An early lollipop handled 18thC wall box from New England holds quills for writing. The table is a tavern stretcher base table found in Ohio. All the chairs are 18thC and were purchased over a period of time and are from a variety of shops and shows.

Pictured top right, the table in the center of the room is a single board scrub top dating it to the 18thC and most likely New England. A horn cup, pewter porringer with spoon and a stack of letters awaiting pick up by the mail carrier, sits at the end of the table. Pictured bottom right, the hanging lantern is 18thC and all original.

As I turned to photograph the mantel, Lovey Makepeace relayed to me the story behind the musket hanging on the wall. "Justus Makepeace, my dear beloved husband, was a veteran of the Revolutionary War having fought with the Massachusetts Regiment and Colonel Wait Wright. After the war, Mr. Makepeace and I settled in Vermont while Colonel Wait Wright headed west and ended his journey in Licking County Ohio."

"Mr. Makepeace and I made the best of our life in Vermont, but the soil was rocky and near impossible to grow anything and the winds blew off Lake Champlain making winters almost unbearable. Colonel Wait Wright kept sending letters back saying how wonderful Ohio was and he made it sound as though if you just threw the seeds around they would grow. I fought and persisted but finally in 1810, Mr. Makepeace and I headed out by wagon and when we got into Pennsylvania, it was the worst ever. There were no roads, just trails with big stumps and I ended up having to walk most of the way. The inns along the way were dirty and crowded. Some of the beds we had to sleep in weren't fit for humans. One day, Mr. Makepeace saw some homing pigeons and he tried to shoot one but in doing so he scared the horses and they reared up, flipping our wagon. All my frippery was scattered about for a half a mile. The trip took us almost seven weeks before we arrived in Licking County to the forty acres Colonel Wait Wright promised we could have. Mr. Makepeace set right to work and before long had built us a very nice little two-room house. It was shortly after the house

was completed that he had a dreadful accident. Mr. Makepeace headed out one morning to hunt with his hired man Hiram Goodfellow. While walking through the woods, Mr. Makepeace tripped on a log at which time his musket piece discharged and my beloved Mr. Makepeace fell to the ground never to take another breath on this earth. Hiram Goodfellow came running to tell me but there wasn't anything we could do. That there is Mr. Makepeace's musket."

Clay pipes stand at one end of the mantel. The small stretcher base table in front is Ohio. Horn cups and an onion bottle rest on top.

Joy purchased the two-piece 19thC cupboard to the right of the mantel in the 1960's but couldn't afford both top and bottom so she convinced the seller to allow her to buy only one piece. She went back later and bought the other half. All he said was "I knew you'd be back".

A powder horn and canteen, made from a gourd, hang on the hook the right of the cupboard and above the early barrels used for storing whiskey.

Lovey continued, "I thought for a long time and kept asking myself "What does a woman do?" I knew I couldn't make the trip back and throw myself on my kin. I thought for a long time about my bad fortune. I started to think of that trip and decided I would make Mr. Makepeace's house into a tavern. It was hard to get a license being a woman but Colonel Wright intervened on my behalf and my tavern has been very successful. Many people pass through Ohio on their way West so it gets pretty busy here and then there are locals who come in from the mill just down the road. Whiskey is cheap too because we grow a lot of corn here in Ohio and since there are no canals, there is no way to get it out. But it does get pretty rowdy in here. Those wagoner's are a rough bunch and when they get into their drink . . . And anyone who is tall enough to reach this bar here, could get a whiskey. See here under this picture of George Washington I posted this note 'I've trusted my money to my sorrow. Pay today. I'll trust tomorrow'."

Dried tobacco leaves hang from branch hooks. Travelers could stop at the tavern and smoke a pipe. When they left, the end of the pipe was broken off and left for the next user. Horn cups and a mix of old and new green onion bottles with wads of linen for stoppers line the shelves. Joy rubbed soot on all the walls to replicate the smoke that would have stained the walls.

Joy has collected for over 40 years and with three children and little money thought that if she kept buying antiques it would make her happy. She started by collecting tools because it was one of the things she could afford. What she discovered was that the trick was to study history and find out what people really had in that period. She made two discoveries. She learned that they had very little and secondly if she stayed focused on the period, she was content. She has stayed true to her philosophy and remains committed to only allowing period pieces in her home. Joy sleeps on a straw mattress in her room on the first floor. An early schoolmaster's desk stands at the foot of the bed in front of the window. Notice the shutters that Joy's son made to keep out the winter winds. They merely rest on the windowsill. A 19thC rush light and candleholder stand on the floor next to the desk.

Over the ladder back chair, the oil portrait is circa 1830 and has an inscription on the back that the sitter was from New York State.

In the center hallway, Joy has hung a heavy curtain that may be drawn in the cold months to reduce the drafts. A small mule chest in red holds a smaller chest and fabric covered billfold. The small mirror with blue frame is one of Joy's favorite treasures.

As we entered the ladies' parlor, Lovey described the conditions once again of the men in the tavern and allowed that this parlor was a favorite room where Lovey could enjoy the companionship of women heading west with their husbands or in some cases alone. Oftentimes, she explained, women used this time to not only share news and visit, but to repair clothing that needed mending. Lovey had a variety of sewing necessities and wools on the shelf for the women to use.

Joy made the large sugar cone on the center of the round tavern table. A banister back 18thC chair sits against the wall under hanging wool.

The portrait over the mantel is 19thC but unsigned. Joy was drawn to it by the gentleness of the face. Raw wool stands ready to be spun on the spinning wheel. Notice how Joy has rubbed soot on the wall near the candlestick to replicate how the smoke would have stained the wall near the wick.

An early X base wooden candlestick stands beside another banister back 18thC chair.

Shown below right, an 18thC chest in red stands below a transitional William and Mary wall mirror.

A basket of comfrey, used to make tea and as a medicinal to heal sores, sits at the entrance to the kitchen. Barrels and a small piggin stand in the doorway as well. Hanging from the beams, a large hunk of smoked bacon dries and fills the room with a mouth-watering aroma. Next to it, a ball of fresh cheese wrapped in cheesecloth air dries and ages.

Joy found the large trencher below the farm table at an auction and believes it came from a convent. Hanging on the wall beside a small early painted wall cupboard, a burden bag holds corn. Joy made the bag, used to take out in the fields for collecting corn, out of leather and secured the sides with thorns.

Joy said she had the small open wall shelf stored for years and never used it, then decided to hang it over her sink that she found at Home Depot. As she said, "you can't just take out all your kitchen cabinets at once", so gradually she began to replace kitchen cupboards with early authentic pieces. A long handled gourd ladle holding soap rests in a small piggin beside the sink.

Having been in the food service business for years and having owned restaurants, Joy still likes to cook and says she hasn't yet found a convenient way to conceal her stove. She does however use a homespun curtain to hide the refrigerator, pictured below left.

A hanging shelf suspended from the beams holds a sack of grain and a storage bucket.

A shed off the kitchen is stocked with chrome yellow barrels, baskets, hanging piggins and small wall cupboards. The entire shed is a collection of wonderful dry early painted pieces used for storage. Joy has spread straw on the floor, which was "tracked in from the fields" and a dry red painted apple basket is filled with fresh basil just picked from the herb garden.

Pictured left, an animal skin dries in the shed hanging beside gourds and Indian corn.

Right, a blue washtub with board stands ready to be used, while other pieces hang above drying. An early barrel with beautiful dry salmon paint can be seen in the back corner.

Stepping through the doorway to the keeping room off the kitchen I was breathless with the ambiance of the room and the aroma of smoked bacon and a burning fire in the fireplace.

An early straight-legged 'everyday table', as Joy calls it, holds a make-do candle stand. The hanging lantern uses a 6-watt bulb casting only a dim light in the room. A garland of apples dries over the fire. A rough-hewn plank seat bench is tucked under the table.

Throughout the room, pieces of wool and clothing dry with the heat from the fireplace.

Below left, the early settle with shoe feet may have been used in a meetinghouse. The weight and small size of it indicates it would not have been used as a pew.

Below right, an early cupboard with remnants of red paint was found in Maine. A trencher filled with potatoes sits on the floor in front of it.

An early primitive ladder leads to the hanging food storage loft. Just barely visible on the wall behind it, an early wall box is filled with cornmeal. Wall boxes were a valuable piece in the early days as many homes were without adequate storage space and wall boxes were an inexpensive means to serve that purpose.

A pantry area off the keeping room holds a double door mustard painted cupboard and a variety of baskets, barrels and other storage vessels.

Pictured below, Joy and John used an 18thC dry sink in red paint to hold a copper sink in their first floor bathroom.

At the top of the stairs, Joy has utilized the space to display baskets of raw wool. A 19thC tape loom hangs on one wall while above the pine chest at the end of the room, an early sampler hangs behind an old basket with wool. Attached to the table is a 19thC swift used to wind yarn. Joy purchased the small child's chair on the floor at a garage sale many years ago for $2.00. At the time she thought it was an awful lot of money to pay for it.

Sacks of wool ready to be spun rest on the floor. The sunlight streaming through the side window illuminates an early six- board chest in red paint. It holds an early winder. The contrast between the dark door, stark white sacks and red chest make this a striking picture to my eye.

Lovey explained that the room at the top of the landing belonged to the hired girl Mary. Because the room beyond it was often used as a guestroom for men visiting the tavern downstairs, Lovey provided privacy by enclosing the hired girl's bed with curtains suspended with hooks and ropes from the ceiling. However, Lovey said it was difficult to find and keep hired help. "Young girls marry young and don't want to work," she said.

A Lindsey-Woolsey blanket covers the early bed in the room used by weary travelers. A rush light and candle sits to the side of the bed and a chamber pot beneath it.

Below an early quilt drying rack holds wool remnants. The shelf holds a variety of vintage clothes.

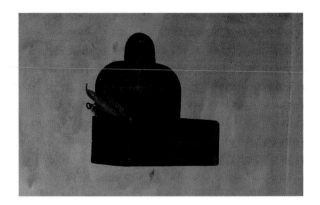

Baskets serve to keep clothes off the floor. A sawbuck table is used as a writing desk on the wall across from the bed. Above it hangs a deed from the 1700's.

Lovey Makepeace had one last word. "Although this is not the life I would have chosen for myself, I have remained steadfast to the success of my tavern as my sole means of being self-sufficient as many other women have been forced to be".

Joy Henson had one last word also. Joy's recommendation is to remain focused and strong; saving money even if it takes years and no matter how hard it is to wait. By doing so, you will acquire a piece which will be treasured for years and you will find true contentment.

Chapter 5

❖

Rick and Vera Flegle

Rick and Vera Flegle have owned their late 1970's home since 1983 and have essentially rebuilt the entire inside while totally landscaping the front and back. In the garden area at the front of the house, Vera has used old grindstones, early house foundation stones and hearthstones out of old fireplaces.

Rick and his son built the cedar shed in the backyard and the working water wheel which keeps the water flowing in the goldfish pond they purchased at an auction.

With the help of a neighbor, they removed the pond and surrounding stones from a landscaping company and built their setting from scratch. Vera personally built the cascading rock formation to create a waterfall effect.

A set of "mix match" ladder back chairs surround an early farm table with scrub top found at Prairie House Antiques in New Albany, Ohio.

A friend made the candle box with carved rooster in the center of the table.

The large corner cupboard in blue green paint came out of Lancaster Pennsylvania. It was a wardrobe in its previous "life" but currently serves to house the television and stereo system.

The apothecary in paint in front of the window is a Pennsylvania find. Sitting next to it, a Steiff bear seems to be studying the primitive tree made by Jane Wallace of Old Mother Hubbard.

Vera and Rick removed all the cupboards from their kitchen and utilize early cupboards on each wall to hold their utensils and food. The wall cupboard is a Pennsylvania piece and beneath it the mustard "highboy" was from Hagerstown Maryland. The inside is turkey-breasted on the shelves.

The hutch table in the center of the kitchen is stenciled underneath and is a New England piece. Although the gray/green dry sink blends with the apple green hanging glass front cabinet, they were found in two different states and at two different times. On the wall to the right of the dry sink, a two-door cupboard holds pantry items.

The hanging mustard cupboard to the left of the
sink is from Ohio. The spoon holder is a new piece and
the box below it is one Vera and Rick made when their
company Call it Country was selling wholesale to shops.

The rack on the counter is actually an old shoe rack
that Vera cut down to increase the space on her counter.

The cupboard at the end of the counter is actually a married piece and one of Vera's favorites. The bottom is an early grain bin and someone has created the top as a make-do, using a divided drawer out of an old carrier.

Before Vera found the green cupboard in Wisconsin that she now uses as an island, she used the heavy butcher-block table pictured to the left of the stove. Sitting on top of the butcher-block is an early tool tray where Vera keeps her cooking utensils with a woven fabric towel. Covering it with a woven fabric towel not only keeps the utensils dust free, but also contributes to the country décor of the room. The hanging pie safe in red was found in Ohio and is another of Vera's favorite pieces.

Many years ago in the dead of winter, Vera and Rick bought and tore down a barn in Circleville Ohio. Rick used the beams from the barn to replace the trusses in their home. The beam work alone took two weeks. Vera recalls standing outside in the cold scrubbing each barn board before an exterminator came and declared the wood safe enough to put in the house. Vera had always wanted a loft for display and when the beams were added and the walls exposed, Rick was able to build the loft over the existing kitchen area.

The master bedroom was able to accommodate the early iron bed when Vera angled it in front of the window. Vera found the early red jelly cupboard in Waynesville Ohio.

Chapter 6

Pat Linton

The small town just northeast of Columbus where Pat Linton has lived for fifteen years was having a carnival during the week I was scheduled to photograph her house. As a result, roads were closed and the detours gave me an opportunity to gain an insight into the quiet residential neighborhood. Parking on the street was impossible and Pat directed me to pull into a small alley beside her house where I could leave my car. I would have thought I was in the middle of nowhere rather than the "city".

Pat purchased her 1900 farmhouse in 1985 and immediately began work to restore it. The one saving feature according to Pat and what convinced her that the house was worth restoring was the original old plaster walls. Pat has added beams in some of the rooms on the first floor and used old boards from a barn to cover the ceiling in the kitchen and build the shelves in the buttry.

When I first entered Pat's house, the first room I entered was a Tavern room complete with a cage bar patterned after one she had seen at a friend's house. All of the walls throughout the house are off-white and Pat has used a watered mustard paint to over-paint giving the walls an aged look.

The husband of a friend secured the two stone pillars at the end of the front walk. Pat topped each one with a stone pineapple purchased at a local garden center.

Pat used the idea of covering the doors with a louvered door after a trip to colonial Williamsburg. The lanterns soften the look of the doors.

Pat purchased the large 19thC paneled corner cupboard as one of her first pieces. It took Pat eighteen years she said to wear her friend down and convince her to sell Pat the drop leaf table. The settle was found locally. The ladder-back chairs were purchased from a New England chair company.

Pat waited seven years to finally acquire the red wardrobe with bun feet standing to the left of the front door. Years ago, Pat had visited a shop which had just opened where primarily glassware was sold. She immediately spied the wardrobe and tried to buy it only to be told that it had just been sold to her neighbor. Pat reports she got in her car, drove right to the neighbor's house and attempted to buy it from him. He refused and she said if he ever decided to sell it, Pat would take it. The neighbor ran into some difficult times economically and called Pat. He and a friend carried it down the street to Pat's house. The magnificent 19thC box on top is a large wallpaper box that Pat purchased at a local antique show. The early ladder back armchair was purchased at the Richmond Indiana Show.

The small sawbuck table with red paint is a New England piece. It holds a pewter plate of pears, a horn cup and an early candlestick. The wall shelf above it came out of a log cabin and was documented as an early lighting board. It dates to the 1800's and is named because the solid board reportedly shielded the candlesticks from the wind and kept the candles from blowing out. Sitting on the shelf are two early tinderboxes.

The cage tavern bar, built by Thom Catlett of Zanesville Ohio, is the first thing you see when you enter through the door. Pat named the Tavern using her maiden name. Ledger books, pen and inkwell and a rare stone beer bottle are displayed on the shelf.

Behind the bar, a musket hangs with a powder horn and a buffalo purse used to carry personal items when traveling.

Pictured below, dried tobacco leaves are hanging from the beam above a small-framed picture of George Washington. A cluster of chewing tobacco is strung and hanging with a broom.

A tri-corn hat, clay pipes and biscuits surround an early whiskey keg on the left side of the bar.

The large 19thC Stepback cupboard is New England.

Pat purchased the early sawbuck table from Ginny Curry of Lancaster Ohio.

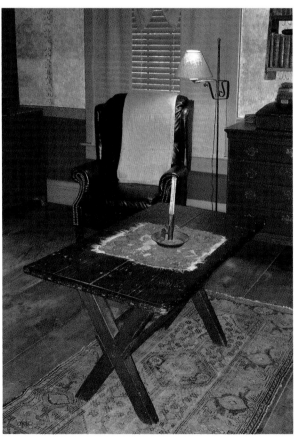

Pat purchased the early oil portrait because the gentleman had a kind face unlike so many portraits of the period. She was able to purchase it at a reasonable price because of its poor condition. Pat learned a lesson and says she'll never do that again as the restoration cost her many times over the original price of the portrait. The interesting early lighting replica was purchased at Curry Antiques and holds a place of honor atop a 19thC drop leaf table with original red paint.

Pat stenciled the walls then applied the watered mustard color paint with a washcloth over the stencils. This picture shows clearly how the walls have an aged appearance.

Pat also purchased the chest pictured below from Curry Antiques. Amidst a large collection of leather books, the top shelf holds a variety of leather and metal tea caddies as well as small snuffboxes.

Each home I visit seems to have an area or room which stands out above the rest of the house. Pat has used this room to the right of the entranceway as a dining area. The mantel is lined with early pewter and a 19thC working mantel clock. The tapered straight-legged tavern table is putty paint with a scrub top. The chairs are new pieces.

Peels, early cooking utensils and Betty lamps hang from beneath the mantel. An early candle box with paint is filled with lantern lighters. Pat doesn't like authentic skins of animals so she has hung a wooden goose to the left of the fireplace opening.

A 19thC cupboard with Spanish Brown paint hangs in the corner over a make-do fireside chair purchased from a shop in New England.

A large open back Stepback cupboard holds pantry boxes and a wool blanket. On the first shelf is an early rush light.

A Stepback with great wear and original paint dates to the 1780's. It holds among other things a standing Betty lamp

Pat searched for years for a folding rope bed and a stone sink. Within a few days she found both! The paint is exceptional on the bed as was the condition. It was found at an antique shop in Kentucky.

Pat couldn't resist the single board bottom and open back bench next to the sawbuck table in her kitchen.

Pictured left, the barrel lid over the small wall cabinet in the half bath hides the electric wiring from the overhead light.

I love Pat's kitchen. It's warm and welcoming and I particularly like the wonderful use of the back splash over her counters. Pat asked Vera Flegle whose home is also pictured in the book, to create the small blocks of wood to replicate an apothecary. Pat then cut the strips of wood and placed them in between the "faux" apothecary drawers. The end result is unique and exceptional.

An early trencher in red hides the sink faucets while a cutting board with great patina covers the sink. Pat's counters are made from old Virginia wood.

Pictured below, the early flour bin below hides the trash barrel. On top of the hanging wall cabinet sits a beekeeper's box. The standing dough box in white paint was found in Pennsylvania. Pat accumulated the stack of large cheese boxes on the dough box from ebay.

Pictured left is the early stone sink Pat had spent eighteen years trying to find. The crock beneath it holds a collection of large strawberry pincushions. To the right is an early pine churn.

Hanging above an early trammel candleholder is more readily visible in the picture below. A gourd ladle holds soap.

Pictured below, Pat's butt'ry shelves, made from old barn flooring, hold a collection of Pat's pantry boxes, which she admits are her passion.

Below left, Pat found the small spice box on ebay. Note the unique small wedding band hogscraper beneath it.

Looking in on the room at the top of the stairs, I'm reminded of an Andrew Wyeth painting. Pat has carried the same soothing mellow tones of taupe to the upstairs rooms.

Skeins of dyed flax hang ready to be spun on the spinning wheel below. Hanging also on the hooks is a tool used to tighten the ropes on the bed and a tool used for yarn winding.

Below right, Pat hired a seamstress to make the bed hanging and canopy around her bed. She continued the use of linens in her room for bed coverings.

In the corner, Pat has placed an early schoolmaster's desk with courting candlestick on top.

Pat stenciled the floor in her room with the same mellow tones as the walls.

Pat found the vintage child's cape at a local auction.

Pat's backyard is a haven for birds. The arbors cover a secluded area for outdoor dining. Used for storage, the building pictured below right is an outhouse built by the husband of a friend. Pat said she added pots of lemons "so it would smell better"!

Chapter 7

Ed and Karen Oberg

The Richmond House, a 19thC tavern located on the original turnpike from Hartford to Boston in Ashford, Connecticut, is the current home of Ed and Karen Oberg. The 'el' off the back, shown middle left, was a stand alone dwelling and the residence of Abner Richmond, the original owner, in the late 1700"s. Land records from 1802 indicate the land was purchased with a dwelling, presumed to be the el in the back. When the road came through in 1812, it is believed Abner Richmond built the large addition and opened a tavern. The home was used only as a summer place from 1900 to 1929 and then stood vacant for almost fifty years when Ed and Karen found it. While the house retained a great many original features, there was no real furnace, one small bathroom and the only semblance of a kitchen was one white sink in what is now the antique shop Ed and Karen operate on the property.

The side door is decorated with a tied cluster of dried blue thistle

Part of the original el, the side door opens to the antique shop. The fireplace was covered with boards and totally sealed off when Ed and Karen bought the house. The settle table in the center of room holds two early dough bowls with red paint and a very primitive earlier bowl.

Pantry boxes and measures with early paint are seen to the left of the fireplace. A grapevine is "looped" over the top of the fireplace.

The large cupboard in early red surface was a Brimfield find.

Off the shop is a small storage area which Ed and Karen have used to display smalls for sale. A dry paint gray bucket bench holds, among other things, a Boswell Hartford, Connecticut salt-glazed jug, measures and pantry boxes. An early wooden rake rests in the corner.

An early long powder horn hangs from a red lollipop handled candle box.

The blue gray four-door Stepback cupboard was found in Pennsylvania. A quilted remnant is draped over the shelf. The large cheese box on top of the cupboard is actually lined with a journal from the 1800's.

Karen and Ed display a graduated set of painted measures, red ware, bail handled pantry boxes and jars in the area which was the original pantry off the kitchen.

The make do chair in the keeping room was made by Marion Atten of Antiques at Hillwood Farms in Illinois and Judi Stelmach of Blue Dog Antiques in Connecticut.

Ed made the large red settle patterned after one seen at Old Sturbridge Village in Massachusetts. The large stretcher base table is a married piece. The top is actually the boards which had been used to seal the fireplace in the shop room

The hanging iron chandelier is a replica of an 18thC piece.

The large two-door red cupboard was made in town in the early 1800's. Abner Richmond's son, Michael, had built a house across the street and when the owners of that house passed away, Ed and Karen asked if they could purchase the piece. Five men carried it across the road and Karen said it might have to stay with the house—which by the way is for sale.

The spinning wheel is also original to the house and was purchased from the estate sale of previous owners.

The basket on top of the cupboard is a stamped Native American piece. The basket hanging on the front of the cupboard is called a quill basket.

A 19thC straight-legged worktable rests beneath an early bowl rack with attic surface and remnants of dark green paint. On the first shelf is a recent acquisition, a very small, hardwood mortar and pestle dating to the 17thC.

On the small worktable to the right, sits a large woven splint tray most likely used for drying fruit.

Shown left, a pine hanging wall box holds three early clay pipes.

Another Brimfield find, the 18thC cupboard in red holds a variety of pewter pieces collected over the years. The early worn trencher above was purchased from The Country Gentlemen in Michigan. The diminutive pantry boxes are from Vermont.

The hinges on the door on the bottom are original to the piece and are called mustache hinges.

Ed and Karen used the original "borning room" to create a kitchen off the keeping room.

The room retains its original fireplace. Don't the earth tones of the hanging drieds, color choice of the mantel and the honey-toned basket create a soothing picture?

Karen wanted the half bath on the first floor off the kitchen to look like a pantry when seen through the door. She asked Ed to build the shelves, and then filled them with boxes and new and old zinc lidded jars. Karen uses a red ware bowl for her sink.

Ed built a shelf to look as though the lantern was sitting on it. The lantern is actually attached to the wall.

Karen and Ed spent months peeling off wallpaper and discovered the original 19thC paint of the old tavern room. The make do chair is another by Atten and Stelmach. Pictured behind it and to the right of the mantel is the original cage bar which Ed and Karen discovered when they were peeling off paper. They noticed that one wall was not the same color as the others and removed the wall to discover the bar. A receipt hanging on the wall is dated 1835 and is for rum bought by Michael Richmond for the tavern.

The small piece of paper is a calendar from the year 1840 which had been painted over. Karen and Ed found it in the bar and suspect it indicates the last year the tavern was in operation.

Ed and Karen dry scraped the tall jelly cupboard, another piece that Ed and Karen bought back from the estate of a previous owner. The 19thC red painted table in the center of the room is unique in that it is both a stretcher base and a drop leaf. The ladder-back chairs are early. 18thC pewter plates and utensils are set on the table.

Karen and Ed have arranged the "tavern room" much as it might have been in 1810. The split gate leg table shown below right has turned legs. Karen couldn't resist the early Windsor chair with a unique shaped back. Above, a small stretcher base table in red is tucked under the window, while below left, a small tavern table fits nicely in the corner behind the large settle.

The candle stand beside the wingchair is a Connecticut piece. Descendants of Abner Richmond presented Ed and Karen with the Richmond family record as a sign of appreciation for having restored the Richmond home.

The chairs beneath the window are part of a group of shield back chairs purchased by Ed in Pennsylvania.

The recessed shelf to the left of the mantel holds a collection of featheredge and an assortment of pearl ware and cream ware.

Pictured below, Alison Shriver of Maryland did the folk art drawings on the mantel.

The large secretary shown left is another Ashford Connecticut piece dating to the 1840's.

Pictured below, an early-unsigned theorem hangs above two more shield back chairs in the corner.

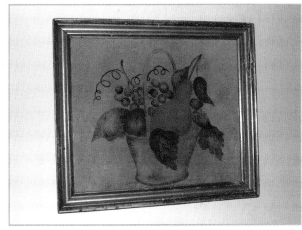

The front door retains the original hardware and half-moon glass. The pattern of the glass is made from small teacups with a heart design. They are original and Karen has been fortunate enough to have found two other teacups should the need arise to replace one of the panels in the door.

The portrait hanging in the front hall is believed to be that of Abner Richmond. It was found on the back of a board being used as a fireboard.

The upstairs bathroom is directly off the center hall landing. Karen didn't want it to look like a bathroom when you looked in from the hall so she placed a 19thC mule chest in Spanish Brown paint straight ahead. The mirror over it is early as is the covered red ware jar. To the left an early rack holds a collection of vintage textiles.

Pictured below, Ed wedded two reproduction cabinets to create a large wall unit which houses the bathroom sinks. Ed and Karen each have their own side. Karen chose to decorate her side with a gold gilded mirror and porcelain jars.

Karen says the fact that the oriental carpet blends so beautifully with the newly made crewel coverlet and canopy was purely accidental. The red painted lift top blanket chest is a Rhode Island piece. Next to it, a unique authentic tri-cornered chair sits under the window.

The 18thC red chest of drawers shown left is made with hand wrought nails. Three of Karen's baskets from her extension collection sit on top. The stacked baskets are both stamped Native American Indian baskets. The bottom is stamped with a unique paisley pattern.

Karen tried to purchase the Lindsey-Woolsey blanket at a show repeatedly during the course of the day and was devastated when she learned it had been sold to another buyer. Later in the day, she was handed a wrapped gift from her husband and as you may have guessed, it was the blanket.

Karen purchased the early chest from a Vermont dealer for resale but then couldn't part with it. Next to it on the floor rests a tool to tighten the rope on an early bed.

The paint in this bedroom takes on different tones depending upon the light. Here the same color looks to be in the brown family. The plaid chair is a new piece. The chair to the left of the mantel is referred to as a Flemish chair but is actually early English.

The 19thC oil painting over the mantel has been passed down in Karen's family and was a gift from her mother.

The standing chest shown below is paint decorated with a feather pattern similar to a Connecticut piece shown in John T Kirk's book Early American Furniture.

In the third bedroom upstairs, Karen has been restoring the original stenciling which was damaged when they peeled off the wall paper. Karen has been using Mylar to re-cut the original patterns and is nearing completion of the project.

Many thanks to the seven families featured in *Welcome Home – Simply Country* whose thumbprints have perhaps made an impression on my readers. As I said in the introduction, it is the people I have met in the journey of creating the "simply country" series which have made the difference in my life.

Special thanks to Lovey Makepeace whose story I suspect will continue in her letters. Just recently she wrote, 'Col Wait Wright, my nearest neighbor, has lately taken as wife, a Virginia widow by the name of Amy Whittle Whipstitch. I expect you have made the acquaintance of the Virginia Whittles as I've been told they are a very important family who has many carriages to do their stopping rounds. Another harvest season has come upon me as I have seen many rotations of the earth. The next two months will bring butchering, candle and soap making, apples to the cider press, corn to mill and woodcutting. I'm thankful that the good Lord has seen fit to allow me the services of Hiram Goodfellow, my hired man and Mary, my hired girl. My candle is burning lowly so I will end this day with prayer and thankfulness for friends like you. Your humble servant Lovey Makepeace.'

And Lovey, I am thankful for new friends like you.

Vera and Rick Flegle, owners of Call it Country

Vera and Rick make magazine boxes, small wooden boxes and specialize in their country thermostat covers. For a brochure or for more information, email *vflegle@aol.com* or call (740)927-0973 or (614)582-6775.

McClellan Elms Antiques

Mike and Donna Perry open their shop in Woodstock, Connecticut Thursday – Sunday or by appointment. They maintain a website www.mcclellanelmsantiques. com and may be reached via email at *dperry@mcclellanelmsantiques. com* or by calling (860)928-0885.

The Richmond House Antiques

Located in Ashford, Connecticut, owners Karen and Ed Oberg open the shop on their property by appointment. Their phone number is (860)429-2495. Ed and Karen's email is *info@richmondhouseantiques. com* and their website is *www. richmondhouseantiques.com*.

America Antiques/America Home Division – Home Decorating

Carl Oliverio's shop, located in Newark Ohio is open Tuesday– Saturday, 10-4. Carl's America Home Division – Home Decorating includes consultation with architects or builders and inclusive interior design as well as customized building of furniture. Carl's America Wholesale Division includes the sale of country accessories, linens and candles. Carl may be reached at (740)345-0588

Criss Cefus

Criss grows and sells bittersweet from her home and each year creates for sale either spoons, ladles or birdhouses with the gourds she grows in her gardens. Criss also sells antiques at the Seville Antique Center. Criss may be reached at (330)628-0917 or by email at *rcefus@neo.rr.com*.